NATURE UNDERC

D0744472

Published in the United States in 2000
by Blackbirch Press, Inc.
260 Amity Road
Woodbridge, CT 06525
web site: http://www.blackbirch.com
e-mail: staff@blackbirch.com

Staying Alive was created and produced by
McRae Books Srl, via de' Rustici, 5 – Florence (Italy)
e-mail: mcrae@tin.it

Text: Beatrice McLeod
Illustrations: Antonella Pastorelli, Paola Holguin, Andrea Ricciardi di Gaudesi, Ivan Stalio, Matteo Chesi
Picture research: Anne McRae
Graphic Design: Marco Nardi
Layout and cutouts: Adriano Nardi and Ornella Fassio
Color separations Litocolor, Florence

Printed in China

10 9 8 7 6 5 4 3 2 1

Library of Congress Cataloging-in-Publication Data

McLeod, Beatrice.
    Staying Alive / by Beatrice McLeod
    p. cm -- (Nature Undercover).
    Includes index.
        ISBN 1-56711-502-0 (hardcover : alk. paper)
        1. Animals—Adaptation—Juvenile literature. [1. Animals—Habitats and behavior 2. Animals -- Adaptation.] I. Title
QL49.M519 2000   00–009438
591.4—dc21   CIP

Staying Alive

Beatrice McLeod

Illustrations by Antonella Pastorelli, Paola Holguin, Ivan Stalio

Series Consultant:
Jim Kenagy, Professor of Zoology and Curator of Mammals,
Burke Museum of Natural History and Culture, University of Washington

BLACKBIRCH PRESS, INC.
WOODBRIDGE, CONNECTICUT

Contents

Sparrow, page 27

Red panda, page 14

Arctic fox, page 36

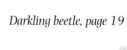

Settler's sea eagle, page 37

Harvest mouse, page 10

Darkling beetle, page 19

Tuatara, page 35

Introduction

Living in the wild requires a broad range of special skills and behaviors. It also requires a lot of work. Animals need to do much more than just find food and reproduce. They must also make nests and dens, survive on their own or live together in large groups, and adapt to changing seasons. This book offers an undercover look at how more than 80 species adapt or fit into their environments, ensuring their own survival and that of their offspring. The book also includes some animals—including dinosaurs—that have died out, and others—such as tigers and giant pandas—that are threatened with extinction.

Bobcat, page 14

How this book works

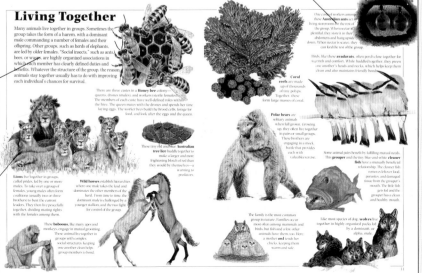

Each chapter in this book begins with a stunning, two-page illustration that shows animals surviving in their natural habitats. These openers lead into double-page spreads with many illustrations, showing a variety of animals as they go about their lives, performing the tasks and learning the skills they need to stay alive each day.

Brief captions explain how each spot illustration relates to the subject.

Vivid, descriptive text accompanies a large illustration that provides a stunning, up-close view of nature in action.

A dynamic, full-color illustration introduces each section subject.

The introductory text gives an overview of the subject.

Detailed illustrations highlight specific adaptations.

Homes

LIFE IN A VAST OCEAN. Like many animals, green sea turtles don't build special dens or homes. They inhabit the wide expanses of warm oceans throughout the world, where sources of food are plentiful. Animal homes in this broad sense are usually called "habitats." Green sea turtles live scattered across tropical and sub-tropical oceans, where they graze on sea grasses and algae. During their egg-laying season, they often get together in large numbers and migrate—sometimes for hundreds of miles—back to the beaches where they were hatched. There, the females lay hundreds of eggs in shallow pits in the sand. After incubation, the hatchlings return to the sea and journey back to their parents' feeding grounds.

Australian **frilled monarch flycatchers** anchor their tiny nests to vines using cobwebs. The male and female birds take turns incubating the clutch of 2 to 4 eggs.

This beautiful **sea snail** (*Architectonica nobilis*) nestles in the seafloor of the Caribbean among other mollusks and coral. It burrows into the sand where it is safe when it needs to rest.

Homes

Many animals build protective homes where they can eat, rest, hide from predators, and give birth in relative safety. Some dens or nests can also be used as storehouses for extra food. Some animals, including many turtles and snails, carry their protective homes on their backs. When danger threatens, they withdraw inside their shell. Other animals build homes in trees, or underground, or in the water. These structures vary from temporary and simple to quite elaborate!

Harvest mice build nests every summer among reeds and tall grass. They bend the stems to make a round nest about the size of a tennis ball. The female raises her babies there.

Beavers build lodges in rivers using branches and shrubs that they haul from nearby forests. If the river is not deep enough, the beavers build a dam so that a small lake forms. The lake isolates and protects the lodge.

Beavers build some of the most spectacular homes in nature. Their dams are permanent structures that can be the result of several generations of work. One of the largest dams ever found was in Montana – it was over 2,250 feet (690 m) long!

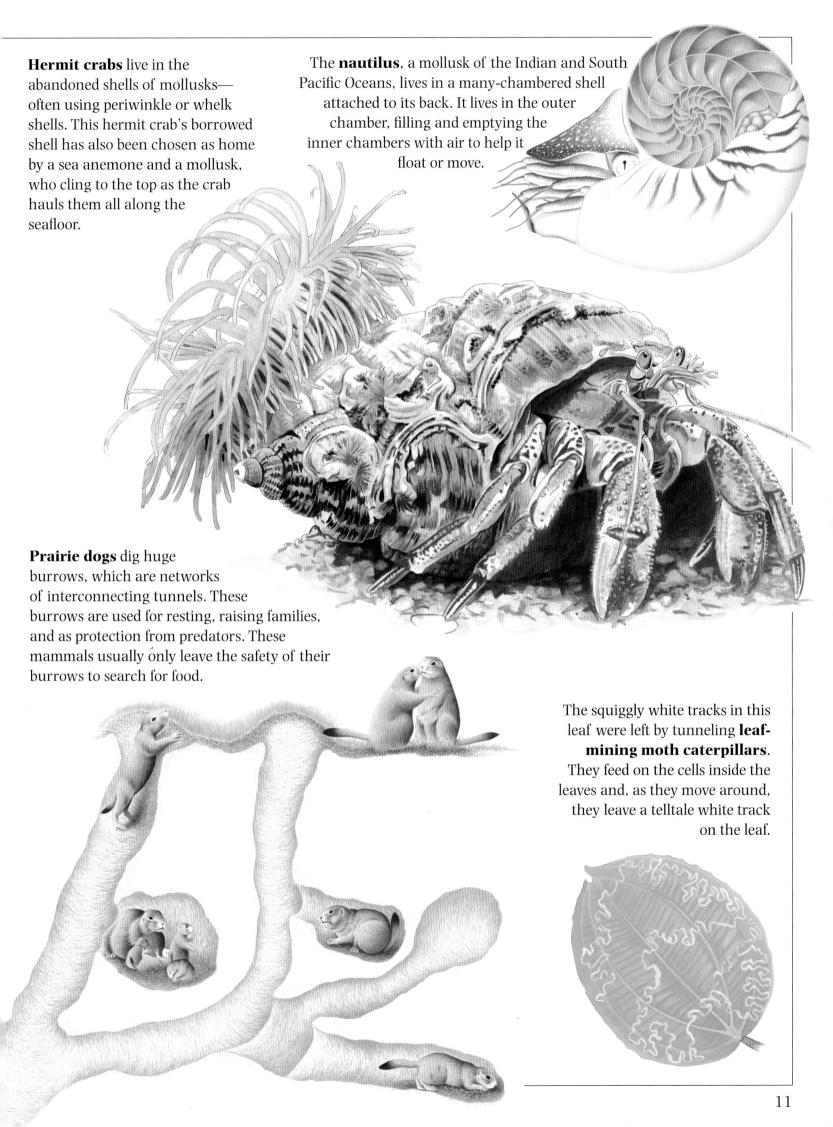

Hermit crabs live in the abandoned shells of mollusks—often using periwinkle or whelk shells. This hermit crab's borrowed shell has also been chosen as home by a sea anemone and a mollusk, who cling to the top as the crab hauls them all along the seafloor.

The **nautilus**, a mollusk of the Indian and South Pacific Oceans, lives in a many-chambered shell attached to its back. It lives in the outer chamber, filling and emptying the inner chambers with air to help it float or move.

Prairie dogs dig huge burrows, which are networks of interconnecting tunnels. These burrows are used for resting, raising families, and as protection from predators. These mammals usually only leave the safety of their burrows to search for food.

The squiggly white tracks in this leaf were left by tunneling **leaf-mining moth caterpillars**. They feed on the cells inside the leaves and, as they move around, they leave a telltale white track on the leaf.

Resting

KEEPING AN EYE OUT. Like many non-nesting birds, flamingoes are vulnerable to predators at night. To avoid a surprise attack, they will keep one eye open as they sleep. Biologists think flamingoes can actually rest each half of their brain separately! At night, these birds rest one eye and its related brain hemisphere, then switch. They also raise one leg as they sleep, tucking it up under their body. Looking at them this way, it's a wonder they can sleep at all!

Resting

Almost all animals spend a part of each day or night sleeping, although the amount of rest needed varies among animals. Sloths and armadilloes, for example, spend most of their time asleep, while giraffes and horses only spend about 4 hours resting each day. Generally, animals that are vulnerable to attack or are high-volume eaters tend to sleep less. Some, such as certain bears, are highly active during the warm months and then hibernate through the cold winter months.

This **bobcat** is having a good yawn. Many animals yawn, perhaps to stretch their cheek and throat muscles as much as to get an extra breath of air.

Red pandas spend much of the day sleeping in the treetops where their brownish-red pelts blend in with the branches. At night, they wake and go hunting for food.

Zebras and other large grassland animals can only stretch out on the ground to sleep deeply if other members of the herd stay alert to warn of danger.

Hazel dormice become dormant in the autumn and don't wake up again until spring. A long, deep sleep like this is called hibernation. After they settle down in their burrows (sometimes with stores of food for snacks), their metabolism slows and their bodies cool so that they need little energy to survive.

Kittens need a lot of rest, and spend most of their time sleeping. Even adult cats spend about half the day asleep.

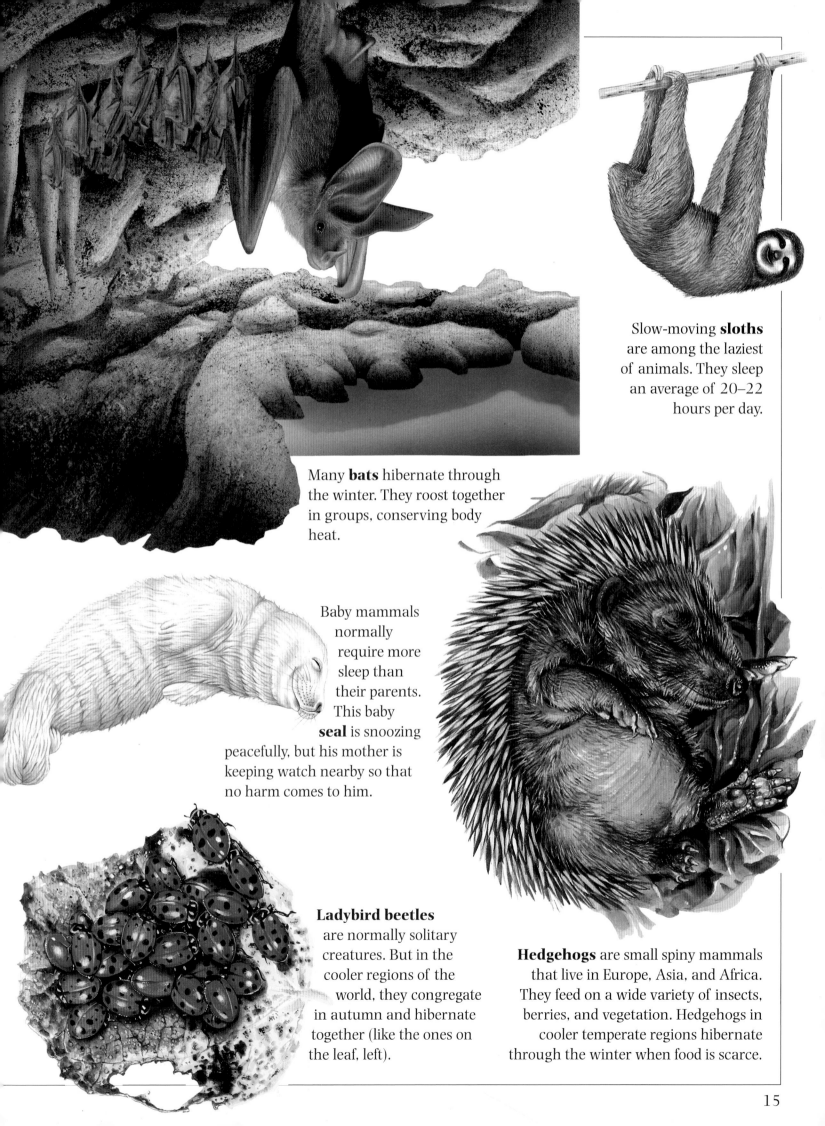

Slow-moving **sloths** are among the laziest of animals. They sleep an average of 20–22 hours per day.

Many **bats** hibernate through the winter. They roost together in groups, conserving body heat.

Baby mammals normally require more sleep than their parents. This baby **seal** is snoozing peacefully, but his mother is keeping watch nearby so that no harm comes to him.

Ladybird beetles are normally solitary creatures. But in the cooler regions of the world, they congregate in autumn and hibernate together (like the ones on the leaf, left).

Hedgehogs are small spiny mammals that live in Europe, Asia, and Africa. They feed on a wide variety of insects, berries, and vegetation. Hedgehogs in cooler temperate regions hibernate through the winter when food is scarce.

Food and Water
TRAPPED! Finding food is the main activity of all animals. Some, like this black widow spider, are skillful hunters that use stealth and deadly poison to trap and kill unsuspecting prey. A black widow spins its web to capture insects. Once the prey is caught in the web, the spider seizes it in its strong jaws and bites. A powerful venom passes into the victim, paralyzing and then digesting it. The black widow then sucks the liquid from its victim's body until all that is left is a lifeless hull.

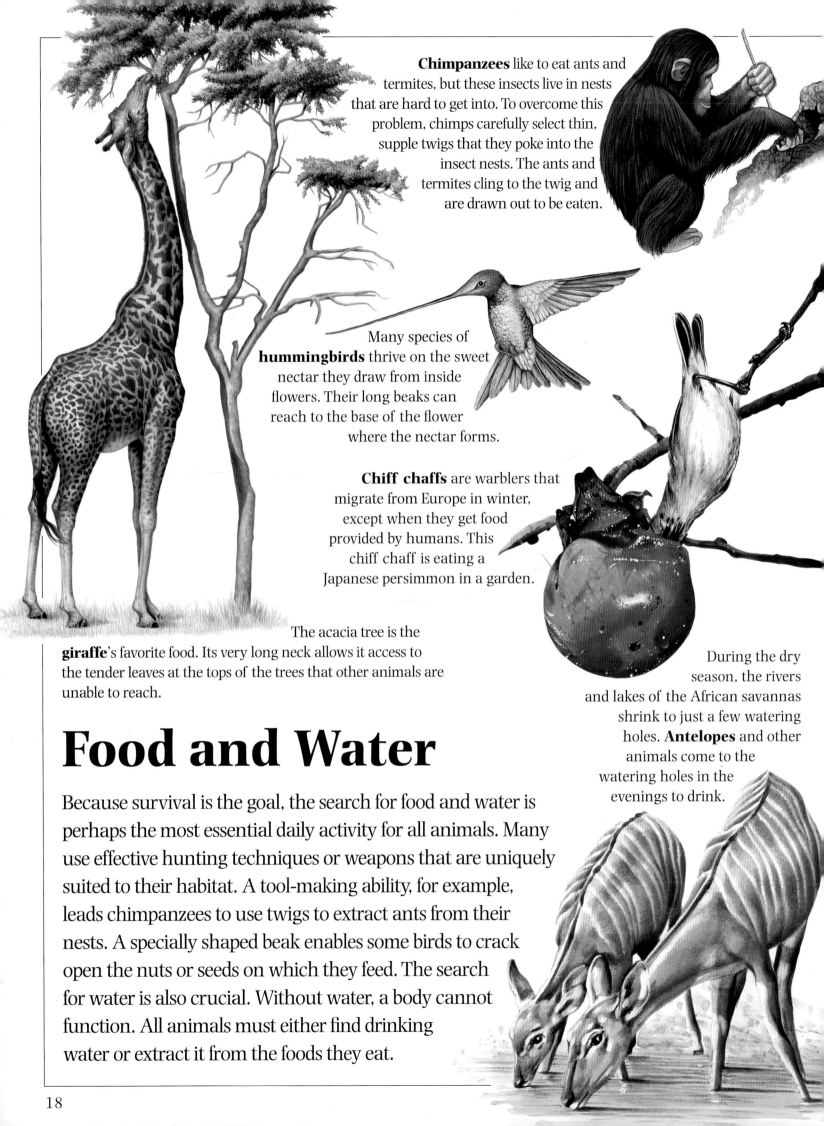

Chimpanzees like to eat ants and termites, but these insects live in nests that are hard to get into. To overcome this problem, chimps carefully select thin, supple twigs that they poke into the insect nests. The ants and termites cling to the twig and are drawn out to be eaten.

Many species of **hummingbirds** thrive on the sweet nectar they draw from inside flowers. Their long beaks can reach to the base of the flower where the nectar forms.

Chiff chaffs are warblers that migrate from Europe in winter, except when they get food provided by humans. This chiff chaff is eating a Japanese persimmon in a garden.

The acacia tree is the **giraffe**'s favorite food. Its very long neck allows it access to the tender leaves at the tops of the trees that other animals are unable to reach.

During the dry season, the rivers and lakes of the African savannas shrink to just a few watering holes. **Antelopes** and other animals come to the watering holes in the evenings to drink.

Food and Water

Because survival is the goal, the search for food and water is perhaps the most essential daily activity for all animals. Many use effective hunting techniques or weapons that are uniquely suited to their habitat. A tool-making ability, for example, leads chimpanzees to use twigs to extract ants from their nests. A specially shaped beak enables some birds to crack open the nuts or seeds on which they feed. The search for water is also crucial. Without water, a body cannot function. All animals must either find drinking water or extract it from the foods they eat.

The **crossbill** takes its name from the distinctive shape of its beak, the upper part of which overlaps the lower to form a double hook. Crossbills feed on conifer seeds, which they extract from the cones. Their beaks are adapted to perform this task.

Food is more plentiful in some seasons than in others. The **American acorn woodpecker** stores food away in holes it pecks into tree trunks. The bird pokes acorns, other nuts, and even insects into the holes where they are safe until they are needed later.

Living in the desert makes finding water especially difficult. The **darkling beetle** of the Namib Desert in southern Africa has a special technique for getting water. When the mists roll in from the sea in the early morning, the beetle raises its rear end against the wind. The mist condenses on its rear and rolls down its body toward its mouth.

Not all **hawks** are fast fliers—many prefer to ambush their prey from the top of a cliff or tall tree rather than chasing after them. They lie in wait until a favorite food animal passes beneath them. When it does, the hawk swoops down on it, killing it with its sharp talons before the victim is aware of any danger.

On the Move

MYSTERY OF THE MONARCH MIGRATION. Monarch caterpillars hatch in the northern United States and southern Canada every spring. By autumn, after they have been transformed into adult butterflies, they gather in huge flocks and begin an epic journey south to Florida, California, and Mexico. Flying by day, they cover distances of about 80 miles (130 km) before resting in trees at night. They even fly over the ocean. Scientists are still not sure of all the details concerning how and why the butterflies make this long journey.

The **Arctic tern** makes the longest migratory journey of any animal. Hatched in the northern Arctic, they fly south to Antarctica for the northern winter. This involves a journey of over 9,000 miles (14,500 km). When winter begins in the south, they fly north again.

Many animals that make their homes in the mountains, such as **mountain goats**, live high among the peaks during the warmer summer months. Then they move down the mountains to lowland pastures during the winter.

On the Move

A number of animals make annual or seasonal migrations. They may travel to mate in special breeding grounds, to better food sources, or to warmer places during the long, cold winters. Some species make incredibly long journeys—the arctic tern for example, flies from one end of the earth to the other and back again each year. Other animals—such as the wildebeest and Africa's other large, land mammals—may only migrate for 100 miles (160 km) or so each year, searching for better grasslands on which to graze and raise their young.

The **American porcupine** lives in the conifer forests of North America. It lives a nomadic existence, always on the move in search of good supplies of the bark and twigs on which it feeds.

Eels in the rivers of Europe and North America migrate to the Sargasso Sea off the coast of Florida to breed. For European eels this means crossing the Atlantic Ocean, a distance of some 4,000 miles (6,400 km). The adult eels die in the Sargasso, but their young make the long journey back to Europe.

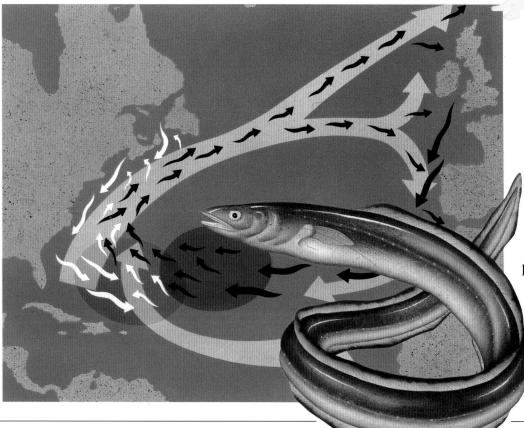

During the non-breeding season, **wandering albatrosses** roam the skies above the Southern Ocean. They spend their entire lives in the air or at sea. Every second year they come ashore to breed. The nesting period lasts for almost a year, because the chick needs about nine months from hatching until it can fly.

Canada geese breed in Canada and Alaska and then fly south to the southern United States and Mexico to escape the northern winter. These large birds (males can weigh up to 20 lbs/9kg) fly in a characteristic V-formation and honk as they migrate.

During the breeding season, many crustaceans, including the **lobster**, travel from the shallow coastal waters where they normally live to lay their eggs in deeper water. As they move, the lobsters will often travel in single file, forming long lines.

Wildebeests (also known as **gnu**) live in large herds on the grasslands of eastern and central Africa. Each spring, the herds migrate over 100 miles (160 km) from Kenya to the Serengeti plains in Tanzania where richer pasturelands provide better conditions for their calves when they are born.

Special Adaptations
BREATHING AIR OR WATER. Mudskippers are strange fish that use their pectoral fins to walk in the mud. At home in the water, they can also spend long periods on land, getting oxygen from air dissolved in water trapped in their gill chambers. They live in swamps, estuaries, and on mud flats, particularly around mangroves. When the tide comes in, mudskippers often climb trees to avoid the many predatory fish brought in with the tide.

Geckoes are lizards that can run up and down slippery surfaces without falling off because they have special sticky pads on their feet.

Special Adaptations

Some habitats are harsh, making survival difficult. Desert animals, for example, must overcome extreme heat, lack of water, and ever-moving sands to stay alive. Some of these animals rely on unique physical abilities, such as storing fat in a hump on their backs as camels do. Other animals have developed features that allow them to live or hunt well in special areas. In most cases, these adaptations have developed by a process known as "natural selection." Through this process, those individuals best suited to a habitat are most successful in breeding and therefore pass on their useful traits to their young.

Gibbons spend almost all their lives in the trees of the tropical rain forests. Their long, powerful arms and strong fingers and toes are well suited for swinging quickly from branch to branch.

Southern ground hornbills live in the African grasslands. They feed on small animals in the dry grass. To help cope with the heat and dust, they have special long eyelashes to protect their eyes.

Desert-dwelling **gerbils** use their long, powerful hind legs to make 3–6-foot-(1–2 m) long leaps while escaping from predators. Their short front legs are useful for burrowing into the sand. They are active mostly at night.

The **camel**, often referred to as "the ship of the desert," has many special adaptations to its harsh desert habitat. It can survive without food for several weeks, drawing on a large store of fat in the hump on its back. It can also go for a week without water, because its highly efficient kidneys can eliminate waste in urine that has a very low water content.

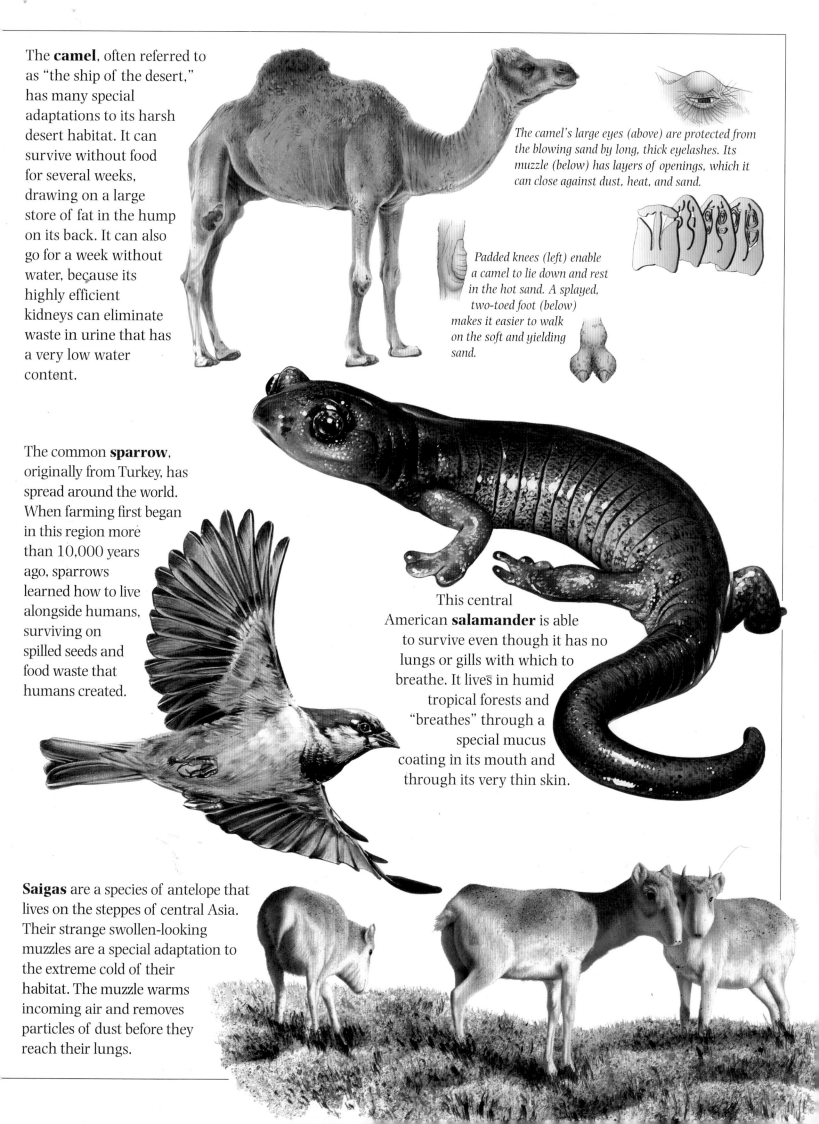

The camel's large eyes (above) are protected from the blowing sand by long, thick eyelashes. Its muzzle (below) has layers of openings, which it can close against dust, heat, and sand.

Padded knees (left) enable a camel to lie down and rest in the hot sand. A splayed, two-toed foot (below) makes it easier to walk on the soft and yielding sand.

The common **sparrow**, originally from Turkey, has spread around the world. When farming first began in this region more than 10,000 years ago, sparrows learned how to live alongside humans, surviving on spilled seeds and food waste that humans created.

This central American **salamander** is able to survive even though it has no lungs or gills with which to breathe. It lives in humid tropical forests and "breathes" through a special mucus coating in its mouth and through its very thin skin.

Saigas are a species of antelope that lives on the steppes of central Asia. Their strange swollen-looking muzzles are a special adaptation to the extreme cold of their habitat. The muzzle warms incoming air and removes particles of dust before they reach their lungs.

Living Together

THE BENEFITS OF COOPERATION. Meerkats, or suricates, live in the arid regions of southern Africa. They stay in groups of between 5 and 30 individuals, known as "mobs" or "gangs." These small mammals live in grass-lined burrows that may also be occupied by ground squirrels and yellow mongooses. Because meerkats are prime prey for a number of animals, one of the gang usually stands on its hind legs to keep watch while the others forage or nap. Jackals and martial eagles are their worst enemies; if one approaches, the guard will screech alarm calls as a warning to the others. Adult gang members also do "volunteer babysitting" while mother meerkats get some food or rest. The members of the gang below are sunning their sparsely furred bellies to warm up in the early morning desert sun.

Living Together

Many animals live together in groups. Sometimes the group takes the form of a harem, with a dominant male commanding a number of females and their offspring. Other groups, such as herds of elephants, are led by older females. "Social insects," such as ants, bees, or wasps, are highly organized associations in which each member has clearly defined duties and benefits. Whatever the structure of the group, the reason animals stay together usually has to do with improving each individual's chances for survival.

There are three castes in a **Honey bee** colony— queens, drones (males), and workers (sterile females). The members of each caste have well-defined roles within the hive. The queen mates with the drones and spends her time laying eggs. The worker bees build the brood cells, forage for food, and look after the eggs and the queen.

These tiny red and blue **Australian tree lice** huddle together to make a larger and more frightening blotch of red than they would by themselves—a warning to predators.

Lions live together in groups, called prides, led by one or more males. To take over a group of females, young males often form coalitions (usually two or three brothers) to beat the current leaders. They then live peacefully together, dividing mating rights with the females among them.

Wild horses establish hierarchies where one male takes the lead and dominates the other members of the herd. From time to time, the dominant male is challenged by a younger stallion, and the two fight for control of the group.

These **baboons,** like many apes and monkeys, engage in mutual grooming. These animals live together in groups with complex social structures. Keeping one another clean helps group members to bond.

One caste of workers among these **Australian ants** act as living storerooms for the rest of the group. When nectar is plentiful, they store it in their abdomens and hang upside down. When nectar is scarce, they can feed the rest of the group.

Birds, like these **avadavats**, often perch close together for warmth and comfort. While huddled together, they preen one another's heads and necks, which helps keep them clean and also maintains friendly bonds.

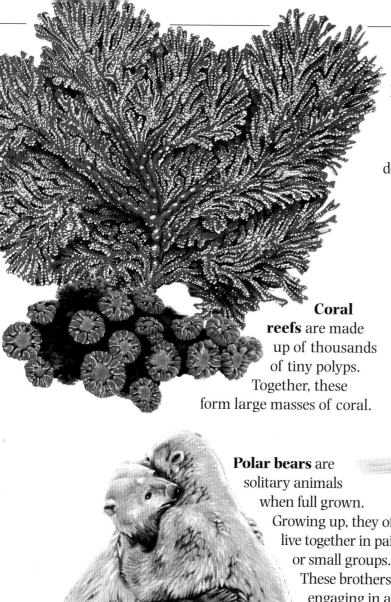

Coral reefs are made up of thousands of tiny polyps. Together, these form large masses of coral.

Polar bears are solitary animals when full grown. Growing up, they often live together in pairs or small groups. These brothers are engaging in a mock battle that provides each with valuable exercise.

Some animal pairs benefit by fulfilling mutual needs. This **grouper** and the tiny blue-and-white **cleaner fish** have a mutually beneficial relationship. The cleaner fish removes leftover food, parasites, and damaged tissue from the grouper's mouth. The little fish gets fed and the grouper has a clean and healthy mouth.

The family is the most common group in nature. Families occur most often among mammals and birds, but fish and a few other animals have them, too. Here, a mother **owl** tends her chicks, keeping them warm and safe.

Like most species of dog, **wolves** live together in highly organized packs led by a dominant, or alpha, male.

Extinction and Evolution

THE AGE OF REPTILES. For almost 200 million years—between about 240 and 65 million years ago—Earth was ruled by dinosaurs and other reptiles. Dinosaurs came in all shapes and sizes. There were huge, lumbering herbivores, such as *Diplodocus* and *Shonosaurus*, and fierce carnivores, including *Deinonychus* and *Allosaurus*. The skies were filled with flying reptiles, such as the long-necked *Rhamphorhynchus* shown here.

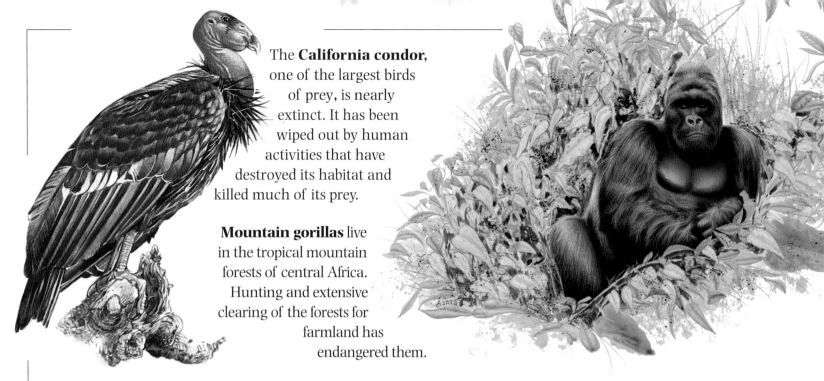

The **California condor,** one of the largest birds of prey, is nearly extinct. It has been wiped out by human activities that have destroyed its habitat and killed much of its prey.

Mountain gorillas live in the tropical mountain forests of central Africa. Hunting and extensive clearing of the forests for farmland has endangered them.

Extinction and Evolution

There are about 1.5 million known animal species living today (with perhaps as many as 25 million more still to be discovered). Some of these species have been around for millions of years, others have only existed for a few thousand years. How long a species lasts depends on how well it can survive in its environment or evolve to match environmental changes. In recent times, humans have altered the natural world through farming, pollution, hunting, and development so much that a great many species have become extinct.

The **giant panda** lives in the forests of west-central China. It feeds almost exclusively on bamboo. The clearing of the bamboo forests has led to a drastic reduction in the number of pandas living in the wild. It is estimated that only about 1,000 individuals remain.

Three kinds of **tiger** went extinct during the 20th century: the Bali, Caspian, and Javan tigers. Only five kinds remain in the wild. Although still highly endangered, recent efforts to save them and their habitats have been quite successful.

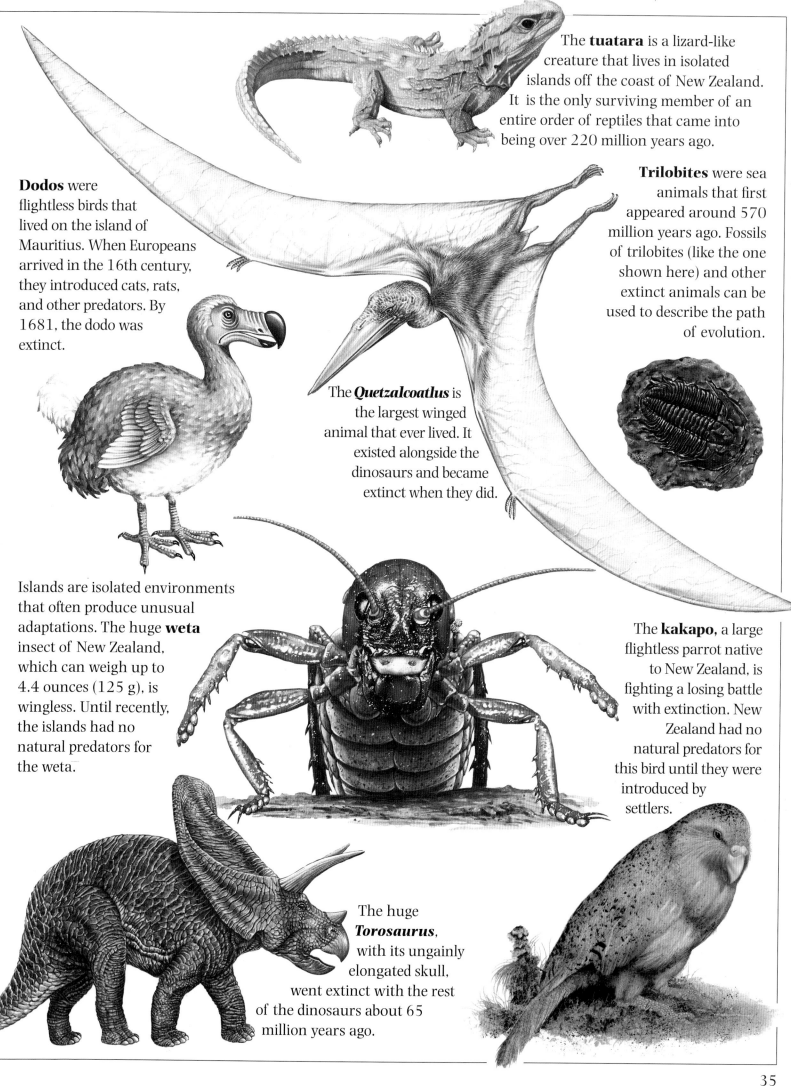

The **tuatara** is a lizard-like creature that lives in isolated islands off the coast of New Zealand. It is the only surviving member of an entire order of reptiles that came into being over 220 million years ago.

Trilobites were sea animals that first appeared around 570 million years ago. Fossils of trilobites (like the one shown here) and other extinct animals can be used to describe the path of evolution.

Dodos were flightless birds that lived on the island of Mauritius. When Europeans arrived in the 16th century, they introduced cats, rats, and other predators. By 1681, the dodo was extinct.

The ***Quetzalcoatlus*** is the largest winged animal that ever lived. It existed alongside the dinosaurs and became extinct when they did.

Islands are isolated environments that often produce unusual adaptations. The huge **weta** insect of New Zealand, which can weigh up to 4.4 ounces (125 g), is wingless. Until recently, the islands had no natural predators for the weta.

The **kakapo,** a large flightless parrot native to New Zealand, is fighting a losing battle with extinction. New Zealand had no natural predators for this bird until they were introduced by settlers.

The huge ***Torosaurus***, with its ungainly elongated skull, went extinct with the rest of the dinosaurs about 65 million years ago.

Maintaining Body Temperature

Mammals that live in cold regions, like this **Arctic fox**, have thick fur to keep out the cold. They also have small, furry ears, that prevent the loss of too much body heat.

All animals need to maintain a body temperature that enables them to metabolize (use energy). This enables them to move around and find food. Animals that live in cold climates have thick fur or feathers, or a thick layer of fat beneath their skin to act as insulation. Cold-blooded animals, such as insects and reptiles, sun themselves in the morning to raise their body temperatures before moving. Animals also have many ways to avoid overheating. Some burrow in the earth, away from the hot sun. Others sweat, pant, or lie in the shade, or take a cooling dip in a nearby lake, stream, or pond.

Brown bears live in the mountains or northern regions where their thick fur keeps them warm. It also protects them from the cold water in mountain streams, where they fish for salmon. Despite their size and weight, bears are actually quite at home in the water.

Reptiles have variable body temperatures. They need to get warm before they can move around quickly. This is why you will often see lizards, like this **Mountain bloomer**, basking in the early morning sunlight. During winter, reptiles that live in temperate regions hibernate because there is not enough warmth to give them energy.

Land-dwelling amphibians, like the **toad** shown here, need to keep their skin cool and moist all the time. If their skin dries out too much, they will die.

This **Steller's sea eagle** has thick, warm feathers that puff up against the winter cold in Kamchatka, in east Russia, where they live.

Mammals, including family pets such as **dogs** and cats, pant in order to regulate their body temperature. They also use the sweat glands in their skin to evaporate water, which cools the skin and helps to maintain a comfortable body temperature.

Many mammals that live in hot places have large ears to help keep them cool. These **Belgian hares** have leaf-like ears in which the veins are visible. They lose heat easily as the blood runs close to the skin's surface, where it is cooled by the surrounding air.

Indian water buffalos suffer in the extreme summer heat of their homeland. To cool down, they wallow in muddy streams and pools. The water not only keeps them cool, but also protects their skin from insects and parasites.

The dangerous **Eastern diamond rattlesnake** lives in the southeastern United States. In the stifling heat of summer, it spends the hottest part of the day in an underground burrow and is active at night.

For More Information

Books

Kaner, Etta. *Animal Defenses: How Animals Protect Themselves.* Buffalo, NY: Kids Can Press, 1999.

Lessem, Don. *Dinosaurs to Dodos: An Encyclopedia of Extinct Animals.* New York, NY: Scholastic Trade, 1999.

Settel, Joanne. *Exploding Ants: Amazing Facts About How Animals Adapt.* Old Tappan, NJ: Atheneum, 1999.

Terreson, Jeffrey. *Animal Homes: A National Geographic Action Book.* Washington, D.C.: National Geographic Society, 1998.

Web Site

Kids' Planet

www.kidsplanet.org

Learn more about wildlife. This site features games, quizzes, fact sheets, and stories.

Index